Global Warming

Shelly Buchanan, M.S.

Consultant

Leann Iacuone, M.A.T., NBCT, ATC
Riverside Unified School District

Publishing Credits

Rachelle Cracchiolo, M.S.Ed., *Publisher*
Conni Medina, M.A.Ed., *Managing Editor*
Diana Kenney, M.A.Ed., NBCT, *Content Director*
Dona Herweck Rice, *Series Developer*
Robin Erickson, *Multimedia Designer*
Timothy Bradley, *Illustrator*

Image Credits: Cover, p.1 Claus Lunau / Science
Source; Cover, pp.1, Back cover, 4, 6, 8, 11, 13 (bottom),
14, 16, 18, 19 (background), 20-22, 24, 27, 31 iStock;
p.6 -7 (illustration) Timothy Bradley; p.9 (illustration)
Timothy Bradley; p.12 (illustration) Travis Hanson; p.13
(top) Alamy; p.15 (illustration) Travis Hanson; p.17 NASA;
p.19 John Shaw/Science Source; p.21 NASA; p.23 (right)
Alamy; p.25 (background) NASA, (bottom) Alamy; all
other images from Shutterstock.

Library of Congress Cataloging-in-Publication Data

Buchanan, Shelly, author.
  Global warming / Shelly Buchanan.
    pages cm
  Summary: "Earth is constantly changing. Although
changes are to be expected, humans may be speeding
up some processes. It's important that we analyze the
data and work together to reduce our impact on the
planet."-- Provided by publisher.
  Audience: Grades 4 to 6
  Includes index.
  ISBN 978-1-4807-4729-6 (pbk.)
 1. Global warming--Juvenile literature. 2. Global
temperature changes--Juvenile literature. 3. Climatic
changes--Juvenile literature. I. Title.
  QC981.8.G56B83 2016
  363.738'74--dc23

                                    2015003156

Teacher Created Materials

5301 Oceanus Drive
Huntington Beach, CA 92649-1030
http://www.tcmpub.com

ISBN 978-1-4807-4729-6

© 2016 Teacher Created Materials, Inc.

Table of Contents

It's Getting Warmer

Earth is warming up. Most of this warming has happened over thousands of years. But things have sped up in the last one hundred years. Earth's average temperature has risen one full degree. That might not sound like much, but it can affect Earth's oceans, land, plants, and animals. This change is known as *global warming*. But to understand the process, there are a few things we must look at first—weather and climate, the carbon cycle, and the greenhouse effect.

Little Ice Age

Earth naturally goes through gradual warming and cooling periods. Between 1300 and 1870, Earth experienced a cooling period known as the *Little Ice Age*. During this time, average temperatures dropped and the world got a little colder.

Weather vs. Climate

Weather is the outdoor conditions of a place on one day. Weather can change in just a few hours. Weather forecasters tell about the possible temperature and cloud cover for a place at different times.

Climate is the average weather for an area or region over time. For example, Montana has a snowy climate. Hawaii is known for its tropical climate. Put simply, the difference between weather and climate is time.

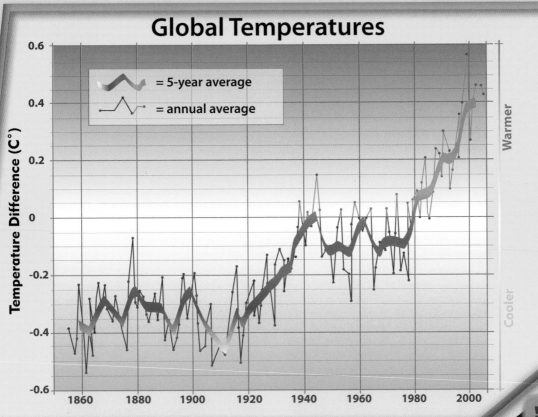

Global Temperatures

= 5-year average

= annual average

Temperature Difference (C°)

Warmer

Cooler

The Carbon Cycle

Every living thing on Earth is made partly of carbon. Carbon moves through the **atmosphere**, land, and oceans. It's always on the move.

Carbon joins with oxygen to make **carbon dioxide** in the air and water. Plants on land and in the ocean absorb this gas to make food. Animals breathe in oxygen and breathe out carbon dioxide. Forest fires and erupting volcanoes release carbon dioxide, too.

Plants absorb carbon dioxide.

Carbon is released into the air by the burning of fossil fuels and from forest fires.

Animals exhale carbon dioxide.

Fossil fuels are extracted from the earth.

When plants and animals die, carbon moves again. It rejoins the air as gas given off from animal decay. The carbon dioxide that does not move to the air goes into the ground. Dead plants and animals decay and compress over time. Some of this carbon turns into **fossil fuels**.

Most of Earth's carbon is found inside rocks and fossil fuels. Moving carbon out of these materials into the air is usually slow. It's a perfect balance for our planet. When people burn fossil fuels such as coal, natural gas, and oil to create power, carbon quickly moves into the atmosphere. This rapid release upsets the carbon cycle.

 Scientists estimate that between 2000 and 2010, the world added about 100 billion tons of carbon to the atmosphere.

Carbon is released from dead plants, dead animals, and animal waste.

graphite

Carbon's Many Uses

In its diamond form, carbon is used for drilling and cutting. Other things made of carbon include graphite in pencils, lubricants for machinery, and charcoal.

The Greenhouse Effect

One reason Earth is heating up is the greenhouse effect. This is a process that happens in nature. Carbon dioxide in the atmosphere traps the sun's heat in a way that is similar to a garden greenhouse. A greenhouse has a clear roof and walls. Sunlight enters, and the sun's warmth gets trapped. This makes the air inside the greenhouse warmer than the air outside. Plants thrive in this warmth.

Earth's atmosphere acts like the roof and walls of a greenhouse. The sun's rays stream through the atmosphere. They warm the ground. **Greenhouse gases** in the atmosphere allow some, but not all, heat to escape. It's a good thing this happens. Otherwise, we would have temperatures similar to the moon. There, it can reach a boiling 123° Celsius (253° Fahrenheit) during the day and a frigid -153°C (-243°F) at night. We would not be able to survive without *some* greenhouse effect.

Ozone Layer

In 1985, scientists discovered that the ozone layer was decreasing in thickness. The ozone layer is the part of the atmosphere that protects us from the sun's radiation. People were encouraged to stop using aerosol sprays, such as spray paint and certain hairsprays. This helped the ozone layer thicken again. Now, new research has some scientists worried that a thicker ozone layer may actually speed up the greenhouse effect!

Lately, scientists have seen an increased greenhouse effect. If it gets too strong, then too much heat will get trapped in the atmosphere. This could make Earth's average temperature rise. Many think that humans are to blame.

Causes of Global Warming

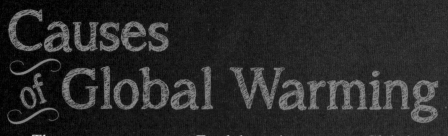

There are many reasons Earth is getting warmer. Global warming is a natural process. But there is a great deal of evidence that suggests humans are speeding up the process at an unsafe rate. Burning fossil fuels, **deforestation**, and farming all speed it along.

Burning Fossil Fuels

People started burning large amounts of fuel over a hundred years ago. This was the height of the **Industrial Revolution**. People built factories and machines. They made goods faster and cheaper than before. Huge amounts of fossil fuels were burned to make these goods.

People around the world wanted to buy these cheaper products. There was a boom in building roads and transportation. This meant using even more fuel. Then, along came the automobile and the lightbulb. Electric power plants popped up around the world. These plants burned fossil fuels to create electricity.

Advances like these changed the world. But burning fossil fuels released more greenhouse gases into the air. Today, we use more fossil fuels than ever before. This may be causing the greenhouse effect to rise out of control.

There is 30 percent more carbon dioxide in the air today than there was 150 years ago.

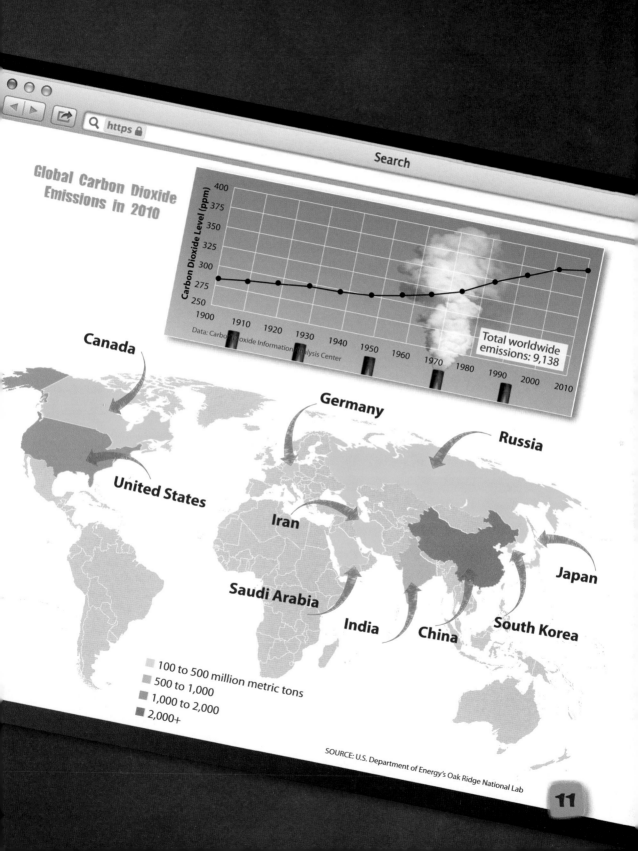

Global Carbon Dioxide Emissions in 2010

Carbon Dioxide Level (ppm)

400
375
350
325
300
275
250

1900 1910 1920 1930 1940 1950 1960 1970 1980 1990 2000 2010

Data: Carbon Dioxide Information Analysis Center

Total worldwide emissions: 9,138

Canada

Germany

Russia

United States

Iran

Japan

Saudi Arabia

India   China   South Korea

100 to 500 million metric tons
500 to 1,000
1,000 to 2,000
2,000+

SOURCE: U.S. Department of Energy's Oak Ridge National Lab

Deforestation

Trees are an important part of the carbon cycle. They help take carbon dioxide out of the atmosphere and replace it with oxygen for us to breathe. They also change it back into carbon in the soil. Trees do this all over the world.

With more than seven billion people living on Earth, lumber is in great demand. People are chopping down forests at a rapid pace. The trees are used to build houses, furniture, and other goods. When whole forests are chopped down, it is called *deforestation*. These trees could help absorb excess carbon dioxide. Now, we have more carbon dioxide in the air and fewer trees to remove it.

Rainforests in America

- remaining
- projected loss
- destroyed

Ecuador

Colombia

Central America

Brazil

Venezuela

Peru

Bolivia

Guyana

Mexico

Farming

With more people on Earth, there are more people to feed. There is a greater need for farms. Believe it or not, the methane gas expelled by cattle and other farm animals is another greenhouse gas. Fertilizers used to help crops grow can produce a different greenhouse gas—nitrous oxide. All these factors contribute to global warming. Although they are not the only causes of the problem, they make it more difficult for Earth to release excess heat.

Effects OF Global Warming

You may be thinking, "So what if the world is a little warmer?" Maybe you like warmer weather. Well, it's not just about weather. Global warming could change the whole world's climate. This could have tragic effects.

Extreme Weather

Earth's rising temperatures are stirring up extreme weather. In some places, rain is falling harder and faster. In other places, there is less snow and more rain. Global warming is bringing both floods and drought. Rising temperatures also create warmer waters. This means more evaporation. It means extra moisture in the air. With more moisture, comes more rain.

Stronger hurricanes are hitting many coastlines. A hurricane can quickly climb to intense levels. This is what happened along the Gulf Coast in 2005. Hurricane Katrina started as a Category 1 hurricane. It quickly turned into a Category 5 storm. This took just four days. Winds whipped to 280 kilometers per hour (174 miles per hour). Waves rose 5 meters (18 feet) high.

Many homes and buildings were destroyed. Most trees were uprooted. Hurricane Katrina caused billions of dollars in damages. Many people were left without homes. Extreme storms are becoming more common around the world.

Lightning strikes are expected to increase 50 percent over the 21st century due to increased water in the air.

STRENGTH				
1	**2**	**3**	**4**	**5**
WIND SPEED				
119–153 kph (74–95 mph)	154–177 kph (96–110 mph)	178–208 kph (111–129 mph)	209–251 kph (130–156 mph)	252+ kph (157+ mph)
DAMAGE				
minimal roof damage	major roof damage	roofs removed	roofs and walls removed	homes destroyed

Hurricane Categories

Hurricanes can be ranked using the Saffir-Simpson Hurricane Scale. The scale is split into categories. It starts at one for minimal damage and goes to five for significant damage. This scale also includes wind speed and the damage caused for each category.

Melting Messes

It's always sad when ice cream melts before it can be enjoyed on a hot day. The polar ice caps and other icy regions melt just like ice cream as Earth heats up.

In Alaska, 85 percent of the state's land is permafrost, or permanently frozen land. But in some places, permafrost is beginning to melt. There are cities, towns, roads, and bridges built on this frozen land. When the permafrost melts, it causes the ground to shift. Bridges and roads collapse. Buildings tilt and shift. Trees and even whole sections of forests slump down. These problems cost millions of dollars to fix.

Increasing temperatures also impact the world's largest ice formations. Glaciers are melting at record speeds. Recent reports show that these ice masses are shrinking. They are losing billions of tons of ice every year.

Ice caps near the North and South Poles are shrinking at a shocking rate, too. The Arctic sea ice is the smallest it has ever been. Many problems are predicted if this melting continues.

Winters are getting shorter! Spring-like temperatures come 10-14 days earlier than they did 20 years ago.

I'm Melting!

Arctic ice caps are losing about 9 percent of their area every 10 years. If this continues, the Arctic will have no ice during the summer by the end of this century. This means that sea levels will rise. And since ice reflects the sun's energy back into space, this also means that Earth will absorb more of the sun's energy.

1980

2012

Disappearing Acts

With changing climates, many plants and animals find themselves unfit for their current environments. It takes many years for a species to adapt. Sudden changes can make it hard for plants and animals to adjust. Some say that by 2050, one million species of plants and animals may disappear. This would be due to an increase in carbon dioxide and other greenhouse gases. Scientists around the world agree with this prediction.

The loss of these living things will impact other life forms on Earth. Animals that depend on these life forms will need to find other food or homes. If they don't find what they need, they will die off.

For example, shrinking Arctic ice limits land and food for polar bears. Polar bears are used to living and hunting in a large frozen landscape. With a shrinking environment, they don't have the space they need. They are struggling to survive.

Polar Bear Population

The polar bear was added to the Endangered Species Act in 2008. It is officially a threatened species. Scientists think more than half the population may be gone by 2050.

The reduction of icy landscapes is a problem for seals, too. These marine mammals rely on ice formations to make homes. There is little area left for seals to live and breed.

In 2007, the golden toad species became extinct. Many scientists think it is because extreme weather patterns dried up the toad's habitat.

Food Is a Must

Polar bears are forced to swim longer distances to find prey. With less ice for them to stand on during these long swims, it increases their risk of drowning. Polar bears have recently been documented to swim more than 48 km (30 mi.) to follow a food source!

The shrinking ice of Antarctica is also a problem for many plants and animals such as penguins, phytoplankton, and seabirds.

Less ice makes it hard for penguins to live and to care for their young. Adult penguins must travel all day in search of food. This leaves their young alone to fend for themselves. Young penguins become open prey to their natural predators. As a result, some penguin populations are shrinking.

Phytoplankton are dying, too. These microscopic organisms serve as the start of many ocean food chains. Both tiny krill and huge whales feast on phytoplankton. But they cannot live in warming waters. The phytoplankton population has shrunk more than 40 percent in the past 65 years.

Other species are struggling because of this food loss. More than half of seabird species have dropping populations. Seabirds eat fish that eat phytoplankton. Seabirds cannot find enough fish to eat. When plants and animals become endangered or go extinct, it is felt throughout their food chains.

Food Chain Reaction

Krill are tiny shrimp-like creatures that swim in massive groups. As the phytoplankton population has plummeted, so has the krill population. Since 1970, they have decreased by about 80 percent.

These krill were caught by people and will be used in products such as vitamins, fish bait, and food.

phytoplankton

Penguin Problems

Penguin chicks are often swept out to open ocean due to thinner ice. The amount of adult penguins that are able to reproduce has split in half in less than 20 years. Over time, if temperatures continues to rise, the number of penguins will continue to decline.

Problems for People

As sea ice melts, sea levels rise. Rising waters are a threat to coastlines. Many of the world's largest cities are built on coastlines. They were originally built near the water for access to trade routes and travel. If melting continues, people may have to move from coastal communities. There will be no way to hold back the rising ocean waters from these man-made places.

Global warming is also causing changes in the atmosphere. In some areas, changing temperatures are causing more storms and floods. Other areas are getting hotter and drier. There, hot air streams are pushing down on the ground and the oceans. This makes it hard for cooler air streams to come inland from the sea. Heat waves are growing in number and length. Some heat waves are lasting for weeks. This causes hardship for plants and animals as well. Overexposed animals and people fall ill and die of heat exhaustion. These extreme temperatures can also lead to devastating drought and epic wildfires.

Predicting Plant Outcomes

Some scientists predict that extra carbon dioxide in the atmosphere will initially help plants grow. After about a year, the effect will slow and then stop entirely. Plants would be pushed out to make room for other plants that are adapted to warmer weather but are less productive.

Temperatures in Death Valley, California, reached a scorching 54°C (129°F) in July of 2013.

Changing Coastlines

Some studies show that if all of the ice melted during global warming, new coastlines would form. In North America alone, Florida and the whole east coast would disappear. San Francisco would become a cluster of islands, while southern California would mainly be underwater.

wildfires

droughts

BADWATER
280 FEET   85 METERS
BELOW SEA LEVEL

California

heat waves

storms

Making an Impact

There are things people can do to slow global warming. In fact, many countries are starting to use **renewable energy**. It is much better for Earth. This energy is not made from fossil fuels. It is thought of as being clean because it doesn't put more greenhouse gases into the air. Wind power is one type of this energy. One wind **turbine** can power one thousand homes. Solar power is also a great choice. Solar panels use the sun to power just about anything from cell phones to cars. Hydropower is also a clean option. It uses moving water to make electricity. Scientists are working to create even more clean energy sources.

But this doesn't mean that the rest of us can't help. Together, we can help cool the planet by reducing our **carbon footprints**. Think of all the ways you can save energy. Put on a sweatshirt instead of turning on the heater at home. Use energy-efficient lightbulbs. Recycle! Recycling can save about 450 kilograms (990 pounds) of carbon dioxide a year from entering the atmosphere. If everyone follows these simple steps, we can continue to move in the right direction. The future of fuel is looking green.

People often use the term green to say that something is environmentally friendly.

Scientists hope to reduce carbon emissions by using iron fertilization. They want to feed iron to algae to make them grow faster. Then, there would be more algae to absorb carbon dioxide from the atmosphere.

A scientist observes carbon that has been captured and stored.

Carbon Storage

Scientists are studying ways to contain carbon dioxide emissions as they leave factories by burying them deep underground in old oil fields. By burying emissions underground, there is less carbon dioxide in the atmosphere.

Public transportation can also greatly cut carbon dioxide output. Ride a subway, a bus, or a train instead of driving a car. Then, there will be fewer cars on the road and less carbon dioxide in the atmosphere. Carbon footprints can be reduced even further if people walk or ride bikes.

Factories use a lot of fossil fuels to make the things you buy. Some people are trying to use less of these goods. By using fewer goods, factories end up making less, and less fossil fuels are burned in the process. Some people are making things at home instead. Others are buying used goods. Some people are even choosing to buy things from companies that have environmentally friendly ways of making goods.

Buses, trains, and subways are types of public transportation.

You can also reduce your carbon footprint when you're finished with a product. Many types of packaging can be recycled. The more we recycle and reuse things, the fewer new products have to be made and the fewer greenhouse gases will be released into the atmosphere. This can help cool Earth and bring it back into balance. If we all work together, we can make a difference.

Driving hybrid or fuel-efficient cars can help lower greenhouse gas emissions because they use less fuel and produce fewer greenhouse gases.

Ethanol for Engines

The cars that race in the Indianapolis 500 are now using ethanol fuel. This fuel is made from plants such as corn, trees, and grasses. A race car using ethanol goes faster, and it is also better for the environment! Win, win!

Think Like a Scientist

How does the greenhouse effect work? Experiment and find out!

What to Get

- 2 thermometers
- 2 trays
- plastic wrap
- potting soil

What to Do

1 Put a 5 centimeter (2 inch) layer of soil in each tray. Place a thermometer in the soil of each.

2 Cover one tray with plastic wrap. Leave the other tray open. Place the soil-filled trays near each other in the sun.

3 Check the trays at the same time each day for five days. Use a chart like the one below to record the temperatures in each tray. Compare the temperatures. What do you observe? What do you think caused this?

	Covered	Uncovered
Day 1		
Day 2		
Day 3		
Day 4		
Day 5		

Glossary

atmosphere—the mass of air that surrounds Earth

carbon dioxide—a gas that is produced when animals (including people) breathe out or when certain fuels are burned

carbon footprints—the amount of greenhouse gases emitted by something during a given period

climate—the usual type of weather a place gets

deforestation—the act or result of cutting down or burning all the trees in an area

drought—a long period of time during which there is very little or no rain

fossil fuels—natural substances made by the remains of ancient plants and animals buried within Earth

greenhouse effect—the natural warming of Earth's atmosphere

greenhouse gases—various gases including water vapor, carbon dioxide, and methane that trap heat in Earth's atmosphere

Industrial Revolution—a rapid change in the economy marked by the introduction of power-driven machinery

permafrost—an underground layer of soil that stays frozen for two or more years

polar ice caps—the permanent mass of sea ice in the area around the North Pole

renewable energy—natural energy sources that can be replaced or recycled by nature

turbine—a machine with rotating blades that converts kinetic energy into mechanical energy

weather—the state of the atmosphere at a particular time and place

Index

YOUR TURN!

CO$_2$ Journal

Keep a carbon dioxide journal. In your journal, keep track of the ways you release carbon dioxide into the atmosphere. Are the things you listed part of nature? Can some be limited or decreased? How can you decrease your carbon footprint?

Searchlight
BOOKS

How
Does Energy
Work?

Investigating
Light

Sally M. Walker

Lerner Publications Company
Minneapolis

Lerner Publications Company
A division of Lerner Publishing Group, Inc.
241 First Avenue North
Minneapolis, MN 55401 U.S.A.

Website address: www.lernerbooks.com

Library of Congress Cataloging-in-Publication Data

Walker, Sally M.
    Investigating Light / by Sally M. Walker.
        p.   cm. — (Searchlight books™—How does energy work?)
    Includes index.
    ISBN 978–0–7613–5774–2 (lib. bdg. : alk. paper)
    1. Light—Juvenile literature. I. Title.
    QC360.W3464 2012
    535—dc22   2010029952

Manufactured in the United States of America
1 – DP – 7/15/11

Contents

Chapter 1

WHAT IS LIGHT?

Have you ever tried to run away from your shadow? Have you ever made faces in front of a mirror? Without light, you couldn't play these games.

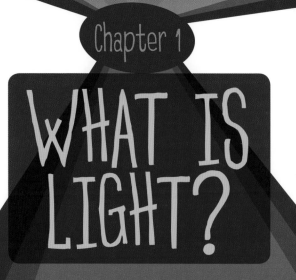

Playing games with light can be fun. But we also need light. Why is light important?

Light is a form of energy. Light lets us see the world around us. Light also makes heat. The sun gives off a lot of light and heat.

Sunlight

Light from the sun makes life on Earth possible. Sunlight carries energy to plants and animals. Sunlight also carries heat to Earth. All water on our planet would freeze without the warmth from sunlight.

Most of our light energy comes from the sun.

Other Light Sources

Fire makes light and heat too. A fire can be used to heat things or to make an area bright. Light energy from lightbulbs brightens buildings and neighborhoods. Some lasers use light energy to cut things.

The red light on this remote controls the television.

Atoms and Photons

Light is very important. But where does it come from? Light comes from tiny particles called atoms. Atoms are so small that billions of them would fit on the period at the end of this sentence.

Like you, atoms can get excited. An atom becomes excited when it gets extra energy. The particles inside an excited atom move faster. If the atom is excited enough, a small burst of light energy shoots out. This small burst of light energy is called a photon.

Everything around you is made of atoms. Air, water, plants, furniture, and even your body are made of atoms.

A photon streaks out from a light source. Excited atoms on the sun shoot out photons all the time. The photons travel in rays. Rays are narrow beams of light. A laser's ray is a moving stream of photons. So are the rays of light from a flashlight.

Light rays move away from their source in all directions at once. That's why the light from one lightbulb can make an entire room brighter.

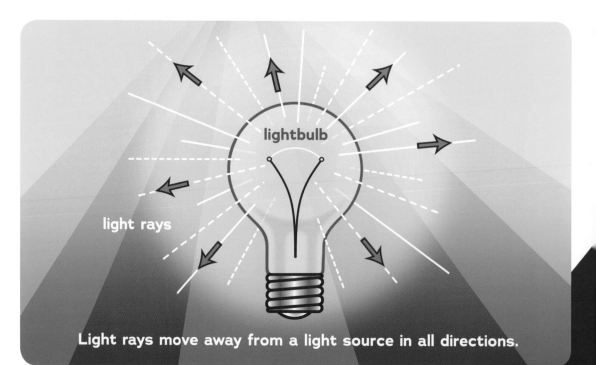

lightbulb

light rays

Light rays move away from a light source in all directions.

Chapter 2

MATTER AND LIGHT

Everything around you is made of tiny atoms that have joined together. When two or more atoms join together, they make a molecule. A molecule is bigger than an atom. But it's still very small.

These kids are pretending to be atoms that are joined together. What do we call two or more atoms that have joined together?

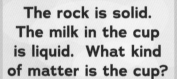

The rock is solid. The milk in the cup is liquid. What kind of matter is the cup?

Atoms + Molecules = Matter

Atoms and molecules make up matter. Matter is anything that can be weighed and takes up space.

Some matter is solid, like rocks and furniture. Some is liquid, like milk or water. Matter can also be a gas. The air we breathe is made up of gases. So what does matter have to do with light?

Usually we can't see light rays moving. But we can sometimes see light rays when they hit matter. You can make light rays visible. How?

Experiment Time!

YOU WILL NEED ALUMINUM FOIL, A FLASHLIGHT, A PIN, A SPOONFUL OF FLOUR, AND A SHEET OF NEWSPAPER.

Spread the newspaper on the floor close to a wall. Cover the light-making end of your flashlight with aluminum foil. Use the pin to make a tiny hole in the center of the foil. Fill the spoon with flour, and set it down on the newspaper.

Usually the light from a flashlight spreads out as it travels. But the light will travel as a narrow beam through a pinhole.

Turn off the light in the room. Turn on the flashlight. Point it at the wall above the place where you put the newspaper. Can you see a spot of light on the wall?

AROUND THE ME

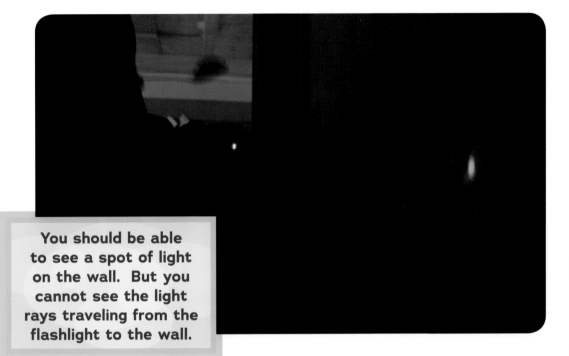

You should be able to see a spot of light on the wall. But you cannot see the light rays traveling from the flashlight to the wall.

Pick up the spoonful of flour. Gently blow the flour toward the space between the flashlight and the spot of light. Can you see the light beam? Yes. The flashlight's rays travel in a straight line to the wall. You can see the rays now because they are hitting the flour, which is matter!

Chapter 3

LIGHT BOUNCES

We can see objects because light rays reflect off matter. *Reflect* means "to bounce off." Light rays reflect off objects the same way a ball bounces off the ground. If an object reflects no light rays, we cannot see it.

Light keeps traveling until it hits something. Then it bounces like a ball. What happens when light bounces off an object?

Prove It to Yourself

Go into a room with a wall mirror. Bring a flashlight with you.

Make the room as dark as you can. If it is totally dark, you won't see the walls at all. That's because no light rays are reflecting off the walls. If you can see the walls dimly, some light is in the room. It is reflecting off the walls to your eyes.

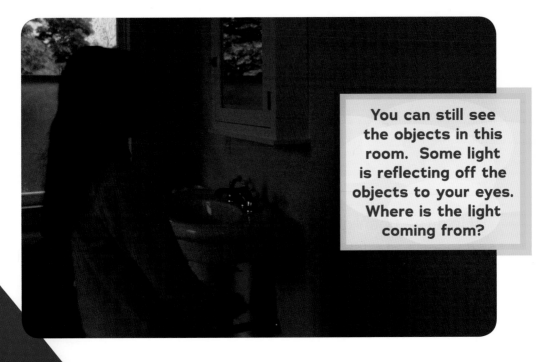

You can still see the objects in this room. Some light is reflecting off the objects to your eyes. Where is the light coming from?

The flashlight's rays make a circle of light on the wall.

Hold the flashlight in front of your chest. Turn it on and point it straight at an empty wall. The wall absorbs many of the light rays. Other rays are reflected back to your eyes. How do you know?

You know because you can see a circle of light where the rays reflect off the wall. The part of the wall that is not reflecting light stays dark.

Look down at your shirt. Is there a circle of light on it? No. Not enough rays are reflected to make a circle of light on your shirt.

The wall is rough. So the light rays that hit it bounce off in many different directions. Only some of the rays are reflected back to you.

Now Try This!

Stand in front of a mirror. Hold the flashlight chest high again. This time, shine the light straight at the mirror. Look down at your shirt. Is there a circle of light? Yes. Why?

The circle is there because the mirror reflects more light than the wall does. The mirror's surface is very smooth. Smooth surfaces reflect a lot of light. Most of the light rays striking the mirror are reflected back onto you.

The mirror reflects enough light to make a circle of light on your shirt.

Chapter 4

LIGHT BENDS

Light shines easily through eyeglasses. What kind of matter are eyeglasses made of?

Some light rays are not reflected. Instead, they pass through certain kinds of matter. Matter that light can pass through very easily is called transparent. Air is transparent. So are water and clear glass. Light rays shine easily through these materials.

Other Kinds of Matter

Some matter lets only a few light rays shine through. That dims the light. Matter that some light can shine through is called translucent. Wax paper, milk, and thin cloth are translucent. Fog and wispy clouds are translucent too.

Clouds are translucent when a little bit of sunlight shines through them.

Some matter stops light rays completely. No light shines through them at all. This kind of matter is opaque. Bricks are opaque. So are aluminum foil and a thick block of wood. Your body is opaque. That's why you cast a shadow. A shadow is an area where light rays could not pass through.

Your body is opaque. It blocks light and creates a shadow.

Light travels very quickly. No matter how fast this car moves, the light from its headlights always travels faster.

Light Moves Fast

Light rays travel very quickly. They travel much faster than you can blink your eyes. Light rays in outer space race at a speed of 186,282 miles (299,792 kilometers) per second. Light rays slow down when they enter Earth's air. Even so, a light ray from the sun takes only eight minutes to reach Earth. A rocket would take many years to make the same trip.

Light rays can bend when they pass from one kind of matter into another. They bend because their speed changes. The bending of light rays is called refraction. You can see light rays refract. You will need half a glass of water and a pencil or a pen.

YOU CAN USE THESE OBJECTS TO EXPERIMENT WITH REFRACTION.

Refraction in Action

Put the pencil or the pen into the glass. Let it lean against the side of the glass. Hold the glass so the top of the water is level with your eyes. Look at the pencil. It appears to be bent! Why?

This pen looks bent or broken when part of it is put into water. The part of the pen in the water also looks thicker.

The top of the pencil is in the air. Light rays reflected from this part of the pencil travel quickly. Light rays reflected from the bottom of the pencil travel through the water. Light rays travel more slowly in water than in air. When the light rays leave the water, they speed up.

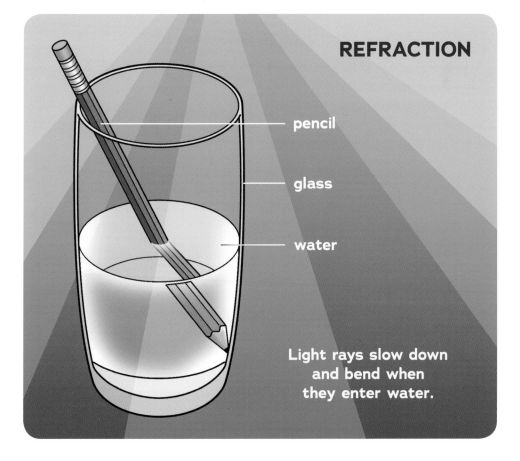

REFRACTION

pencil

glass

water

Light rays slow down
and bend when
they enter water.

The rays bouncing off the bottom of the pencil are refracted as they speed up. The rays change direction and make the pencil seem bent. But if you pull the pencil out of the glass, you can see that it isn't bent.

The pen looks straight when it is not in the water. The light rays bouncing off the pen are no longer refracted.

Chapter 5

COLORS

Sunlight is called white light. But white light contains many different colors mixed together. It has all the colors in the rainbow! A simple experiment will help you prove this.

Light might look white. But it is really made up of many colors. What kind of light is made up of every color?

Each color of light has a different wavelength. Blue light has a short wavelength. Red light has the longest wavelength. Each color of wave is refracted a different amount.

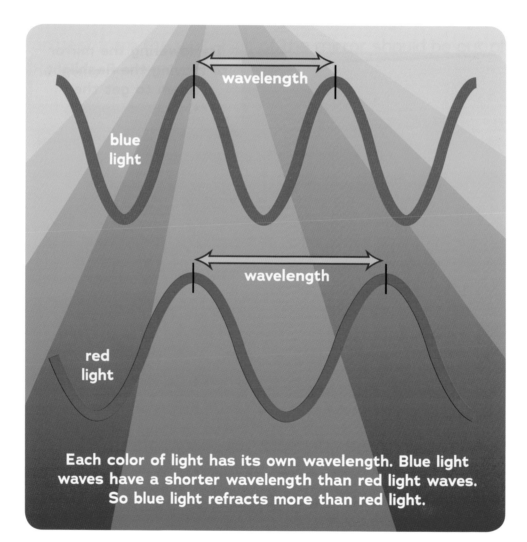

wavelength

blue light

wavelength

red light

Each color of light has its own wavelength. Blue light waves have a shorter wavelength than red light waves. So blue light refracts more than red light.

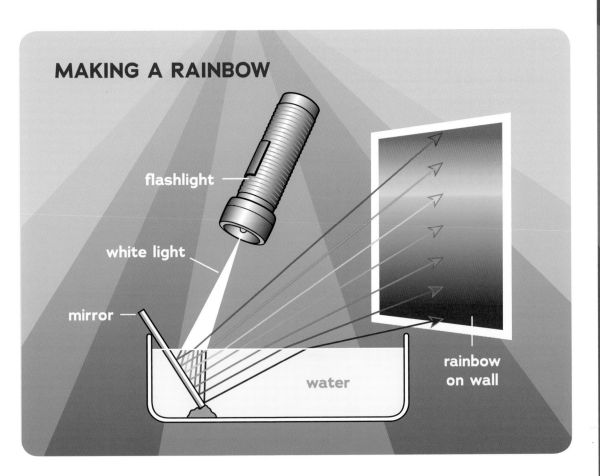

MAKING A RAINBOW

flashlight

white light

mirror

water

rainbow on wall

When white light travels into the water, all the light waves are refracted. Each wavelength of light bends different amounts. This separates the white light into colors. Then the mirror reflects the waves to the wall. Our eyes see them as separate colors. We can see all the colors at once. We see a rainbow.

Objects Have Different Colors

Each object absorbs and reflects light waves differently. Because of this, objects have different colors. When an object reflects all light waves, it looks white.

When you see a red apple, you are seeing red light waves. The apple reflects red light waves. Light waves of other colors are absorbed into the apple.

You see a red apple because all the colors except red are absorbed into the apple. Red light is reflected from the apple's skin.

Chapter 6

LIGHT AND HEAT

When an object absorbs all colors of light, it looks black. What happens to matter when light waves are absorbed? When light rays are absorbed, they make matter get hot.

When you are outside on a sunny day, you will feel warmer wearing a black shirt than wearing a white one. Do you know why?

Experiment Time Again!

You can prove this with four sheets of paper, two white and two black. You'll also need tape, a scissors, a thermometer, water, and two identical glasses.

> For this experiment, use two glasses that are the same. If the glasses are different, the experiment won't work as well.

Fill both glasses with cool water. Take the temperature of the water in each glass. Write down the temperatures. The water in both glasses should be about the same temperature.

Wrap one glass with white paper. Cover the top of the glass with a small piece of white paper. Do the same thing to the other glass using the black paper.

Put the glasses next to each other in direct sunlight. Wait thirty minutes. Take the temperature of the water in each glass. Have the temperatures changed?

Do this experiment in the middle of the day. The sun's rays shine brightest then.

Absorbing and Refracting Rays

The water in the glass covered with black paper is much warmer. Why? The black paper has absorbed all the light rays. The absorbed rays heated the water.

The water in the glass covered with white paper hasn't heated up as much. Why? The white paper reflected most of the light rays. Fewer rays were absorbed. So the water didn't get as warm as the water in the other glass.

The white paper reflected most of the light rays.

You have learned a lot about light. Sunlight warms Earth. Light brightens a dark place. It adds color to your life. The next time you look in a mirror, think of light. Without it, your reflection wouldn't be there!

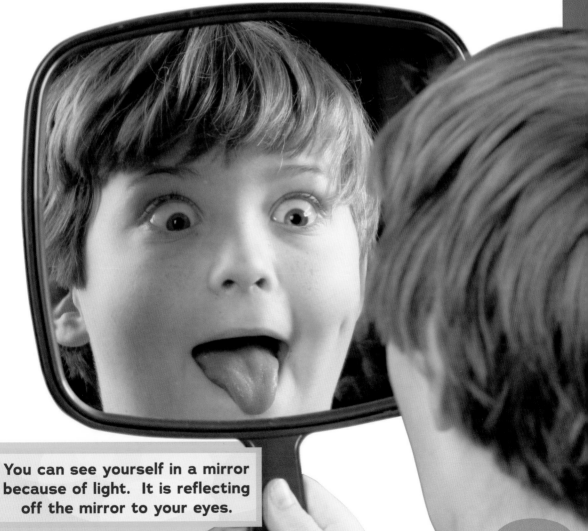

You can see yourself in a mirror because of light. It is reflecting off the mirror to your eyes.

Glossary

absorb: to soak up or take in

atom: a very tiny particle that makes up all things

energy: the ability to do work

matter: anything that can be weighed and takes up space. Matter can be a solid, a liquid, or a gas.

molecule: a group of atoms that are joined together

opaque: blocking light rays completely

photon: a tiny packet of light energy

ray: a narrow beam of light

reflect: to bounce off matter

refraction: the bending of light as it passes from one material to another

translucent: letting some light pass through, but not all

transparent: lets all light pass through so that objects on the other side can be seen clearly

wavelength: the distance on a wave from one top point to the next top point

Learn More about Light

Books

Ballard, Carol. *Exploring Light*. New York: PowerKids Press, 2008. This book explains where light comes from, how light travels, and how we see.

Cook, Trevor. *Experiments with Light and Sound*. New York: PowerKids Press, 2009. Hands-on experiments teach all about light and sound.

Stille, Darlene R. *Light*. Chanhassen, MN: Child's World, 2005. Learn about how light moves, the colors of light, and how we use light.

Walker, Sally M. *Investigating Electricity*. Minneapolis: Lerner Publications Company, 2012. Explore electricity and its connection to light in this informative book.

Websites

BBC Bitesize Science: Light and Shadows
http://www.bbc.co.uk/schools/ks2bitesize/science/physical_processes/light_shadows/play.shtml
This website features fun games related to light and shadows.

Dragonfly TV: Light and Color
http://pbskids.org/dragonflytv/show/lightandcolor.html
Watch a movie showing how five students used light and color to complete a project for their school's science club, and read about how you can experiment with light and color.

The NASA SCI Files: Light and Color
http://scifiles.larc.nasa.gov/text/kids/Problem_Board/problems/light/sim1.html
This useful site explains how and why we see different colors.

Index

Photo Acknowledgments

All images provided by Andy King except for the following: © Rubberball/Mark Andersen/Getty Images, cover; © Feverpitched/Dreamstime.com, p. 32. Illustrations by © Laura Westlund/ Independent Picture Service.

Main body text set in Adrianna Regular 14/20.
Typeface provided by Chank.